W9-CRP-654

AuthorHouse™
1663 Liberty Drive
Bloomington, IN 47403
www.authorhouse.com
Phone: 1 (800) 839-8640

Published by AuthorHouse 11/12/2015

ISBN: 978-1-5049-5786-1 (sc)
ISBN: 978-1-5049-5787-8 (e)

authorHOUSE®

CONTENTS

INTRODUCTION

These are some of the many gifts from my heart and soul, my Spirit. I did not know where they came from when poetry began to flow through me after the sudden death of my mother when I was 12 year's old. I now realize that it was that unbearable emotional shock that opened this avenue of inspiration to me. It is my *JOY* to share these with you, for they belong to all of us

To receive these inspirations (In-Spirit-ations) into *YOUR* soul & let them assist you in the opening of the heart center of LOVE, it is best to:

READ THEM SLOWLY AND LET THEM IN ONE LINE AT A TIME.

READ THEM OUT-LOUD ALONE, OR WITH ANOTHER PERSON.

TO EXPERIENCE A FULL BOUQUET OF INSPIRATION,
IF ONLY ONE HAS FILLED UP YOUR SOUL, REST THERE.

PERHAPS ANOTHER POEM, PRAYER OR WISDOM ANOTHER DAY
WILL FEED YOU AGAIN AND THERE WILL BE MORE ROOM
TO LET IT IN.

REMEMBER TO COME BACK TO THE OASIS OFTEN
TO GIVE THE SOUL ANOTHER DRINK.

~ Iris Arla Moore

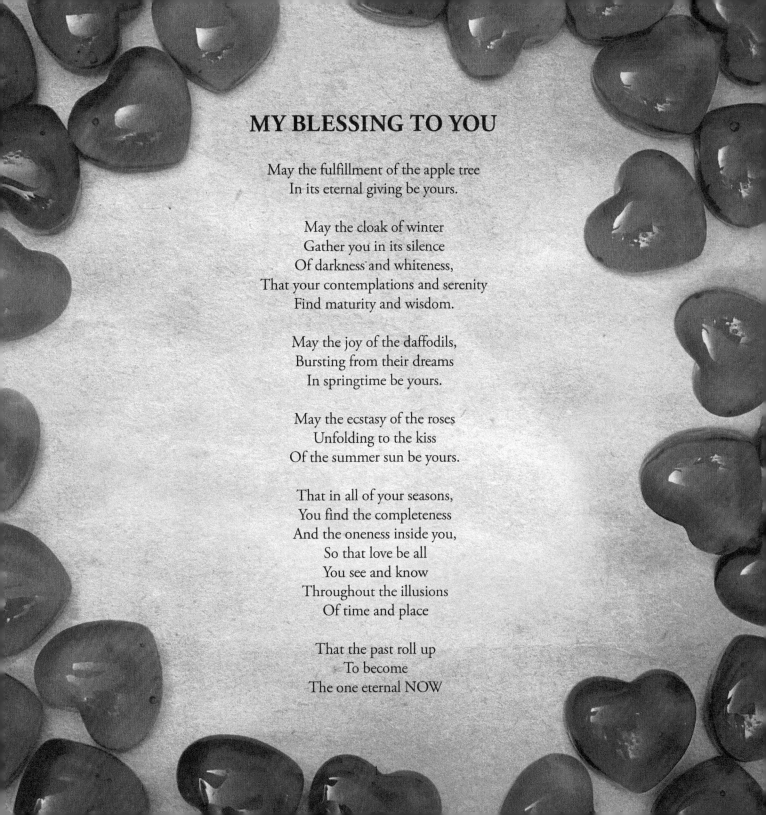

MY BLESSING TO YOU

May the fulfillment of the apple tree
In its eternal giving be yours.

May the cloak of winter
Gather you in its silence
Of darkness and whiteness,
That your contemplations and serenity
Find maturity and wisdom.

May the joy of the daffodils,
Bursting from their dreams
In springtime be yours.

May the ecstasy of the roses
Unfolding to the kiss
Of the summer sun be yours.

That in all of your seasons,
You find the completeness
And the oneness inside you,
So that love be all
You see and know
Throughout the illusions
Of time and place

That the past roll up
To become
The one eternal NOW

FROM A WINTER'S DREAM

It's the golden laughter

And the green joy

Dancing into my brain

Through the windows of my soul,

As little rain feet

Walk on my head

And race down my face.

I see rainbow blossoms

Where the wind is making love

To the willow tree

In this jubilant now

Of life awakening

From a winter's dream.

JOYFUL SPRING

Joyful spring!
The buds appear
Upon the barren branches now.
The season of promise blesses the land.
Life awakens to the songbird's call,
As I reach out to touch the Earth.

The oak tree stirs
Within the acorn's tiny heart.
Spring has left her footprints everywhere.
I kneel before a gentle violet flower.
My soul feels lighter,
Beauty touched just now.

The flower of my love
Opens in response within my soul.
So beautiful has Earth Mother
Made the spring this year,
That I cannot move.
She holds me captive
In this eternal hour.

SURRENDER

Surrendered
    Are the seeds
    Lying gently in the Earth,
    Being and knowing
    The rain and sun will bring
    Their splendid dreams to birth.

Surrendered
    Is the caterpillar
    To the strange call within
    To spin a cocoon
    And be re-shaped;
    To never go back again.

Surrendered
    Is the butterfly
    To its wings of destiny…
    That Love will hold it
    In its flight
    As it sees things differently.

Surrendered am I
    In the bosom of Love
    That carries me without fear,
    So I can know
    The fullness of life
    And all that my Spirit holds dear.

YOUNG AGAIN

When life is young and raspberry

And time turns only

To the tune of the summer...

When bare feet go walking

On paths that go nowhere,

And thoughts are of sunshine

And the warm lazy river,

Then I know

I shall always be

Young again.

EARTH MOTHER

Earth Mother,
Your caresses are more beautiful
Than any I have known until now.
Until now, I did not feel our oneness.
I did not know your mother love.
Now I hug your cedar trees,
Play in your dancing streams
And hear the rocks singing
Of the oneness of all things.

Your winds refresh and cleanse me.
I touch your body
And feel the union of Great Spirit's Love
With you, my Earth Mother.

Your mountains call me
Where the great rivers flow from your bosom.
Your trees lift me to the sun
Where I melt into the forever sky.

Earth Mother,
Help me keep my roots firm,
But let my Spirit soar like an eagle…
That our light and love merge in the oneness
Of the Great Spirit
Here in your womb
Earth Mother.

HIKER'S PRAYER

Wild gushing water fall
Sprays my hot body
With its cool water...
Helps me feel free.

Lush fruitful forest,
Deep winding river...
Wild is the life you give,
Green, free and wild.

Indian Paintbrush
And bright yellow buttercups
Grow unmolested
On your mossy floor.

I shall walk gently
And embrace your spirit,
Leaving my blessing
With each step I take...

And pray that forever
No one will rape
Your virgin beauty,
Your pure free soul.

FAIRY DREAMS

Fairy wishes, fairy dreams…
You can find them
Under rocks and in the streams,
For they still dance in forests deep
Upon a winding path
Into your sleep.

They sprinkle star dust on your toes
And in your eyes,
And sometimes in your nose,
So you can dance with them
Into the starlit skies
Beyond the sunset into the sunrise.

THANK YOU

Because you are there,
My pain dissolves into a pool of tears.
My soul touches the greening grass
Beneath my feet.
The barren tree
Gathers the sun in its arms,
As I see Silhouettes of hope
Against a January sky.

APOLOGY

I did not intend to leave you for so long
But I have been on a long journey
Releasing pain…
A journey I had to make alone.

Now I am no longer in a cocoon…
I am a butterfly
With freedom in my wings!

Come fly with me.

Beloved,

In my longing
There is a day like this one,
Where I can bask in beauty with you...
The summer splendor in our hearts,
Barefoot on the grass
By the water's edge.

Beloved One...

Who holds the blue forever
In your eyes,
Blessed are we...
For it is easy
To see God there.

FOR HELEN

Through the windows of your life
May happy bluebirds fly
Over paths where roses bloom
Against a peaceful sky.

May love, like petals from the rose,
Fill days with joy and laughter
So even dark clouds run away,
With sunshine chasing after.

A GIFT OF PEACE

A gift of peace you gave me
Dearest friend,
As I felt the calm embrace
Within your eyes.

The absence of tears and tensions
Left you open.
My soul reached out to touch your freedom...
To know the secret carried in the calmness
Of your lovely face.

It said more than anything
That I have heard or read.
It nestled down into my soul
And rested there.

Now whenever I think of you,
That thought still brings
Your gift of peace.

With the mortar of my tears,
I rebuild my life
Brick by brick
And step by step.

How long, O God
Have I looked through
Glasses streaked with pain
At a world I saw as separate
From myself?

How many rivers of Love
Have You poured over me
Before I could see, trust, and surrender
To the Love You really are in me
And everyone?

PASSAGE

When in the emptiness of loved ones gone,
Comes the bud of spring
And the swallow's song…

When from the mountain's splendor
I can see
Summer after rain…

When from the valley's portals
I feel joy after pain,
Then I know that in my soul

God still reigns.

The grasses growing in the sand by the ocean
Are firm and strong because they have endured
The powerful ocean winds and waves
That force their way through them,
And their roots are deep in the sand.

So is my love for You my God,
Even when the harsh winds of adversity
Blow through my soul.

I have planted seeds of laughter
In many a garden.
Like a scarecrow,
They chase away the man-made illusions
Of pain and sorrow.

WITH THANKS TO THE MASTER

The cold winds have come
With the storms of December,
And you have appeared
On the edge of my dreaming.

In the winter of my waking,
You have laughed in the night.
You have sent all the shadows
To dance in the garden
And fade away softly
At the call of the dawn.

"Awake from your dreaming,"
I hear your voice calling,
"And come to the garden.
Look into the pond,
And notice the joy
Has returned to the faces
You wore in the dreaming
That you were not love."

HOPE

Hope awakens in every flower...

Light shines from within.

Let us lift up our hearts

To the place where we all first began.

Let our light shine

On the darkening clouds.

Let it dispel any fear...

Love is complete in the soul that sings,

Knowing that God is there.

ILLUSIONS

Illusions are like shadows

That move in and out of dreams.

We are the great pretenders;

The inventors of our schemes.

When the winds of love

Finally blow the past away,

We will find the joy

That loving brings today.

FREEDOM

I walk by the ocean… The breakers high
Reflect the blue of the sunlit sky.

I see my footprints where I stand,
Pressed for moments in the sand.

I hear the water's mighty roar
And watch the graceful seagull soar…

And I thank my God for life so free
As I walk alone beside the sea.

ONENESS

I am ocean
I am sky
I am the wind passing me by
I am the sun
The starry night
For all are inside my mind in flight

THE GIFT

Tiny buds in the snow,
Quiescent and mellow…
The Crocus are blooming,
So small, proud and yellow.
Their little feet stretch
To call forth the spring.
From my soul I now send you
This pure golden thing.

UNTIL I REMEMBER

Let me rest beside you, lovely flower
And learn of your secrets and ancient wisdom.

Let me BE here
By your peaceful beingness,
Your intoxicating fragrance and beauty,

Until I remember who I am.

CREATION

Every picture that is painted,

Every song that's ever sung,

Everything that has been written,

Every dance once begun

Is a gift to all Creation,

Whether or not they see…

For everyone is in and part

Of all that has come to be.

I wish you
Infinite *JOY* and *HAPPINESS*,
With *LOVE* *fully expressed*
In the Divine caress
Of this Celebration Day.

SEASONS OF LOVE

The snow lies cold and heavy on the ground,
The sun reflecting beauty's quiet sound…
While underneath the snow
The hopes of spring will grow
Into the gentle flowers of Love.

The snow is melting into mountain streams,
Filling the river beds with ocean dreams.
Listen to the song
As it travels on:
"Your cup shall overflow with Love."

The Meadowlark is in the summer sky…
She is not alone; her mate's nearby.
The warming summer breeze
Whispers through the trees,
"Neither shall you want for Love."

The trees are dressed in regal splendor now…
The harvest ripe and heavy on the bough.
Listen to what they say,
"There's no other way;
Come and share the fruits of my Love."

WHAT IS LOVE ?

Love is the laughter we cannot deny,
The healing that happens
When we give up the "try,"
And know God is in everything
No matter what life brings.

God-in-me-can is true.
Love is truth.
Love is a song that sets me free
From thoughts that have imprisoned me.
Love is the light that never goes out,
For love is all
And all is love,
And that's what life's about.

LOVE IS

Love is the welcomed Sun
Awakening the dawn;
To know that all are one
under its canopy,

Love is a flower
Opening to the sun…
To know its golden hour
In full splendor.

Love is the melody
Carried on the wind
To comfort the baby
In its crying.

Love is joy realized;
A mother embracing her child
In unlimited surprise
As love deepens.

Love is Mother Earth,
Giving her bounty to all…
To bring forth a new birth
Of Creation.

For Love IS
ALL.

My God,

I celebrate my *LOVE* for You…

I celebrate my dreams come true.

I'm grateful I can be

Everything that you are in me

And to know Your Love is true,

As I celebrate Your Love,

And I celebrate my Love

For You.

MORNING PRAYER

O Guardian Mother,
O Blessed Father,

What shall we do today?
Let me rest in your arms…
Let me awaken in Your Love.

O my God, let there be
Full awareness of you
Masquerading as me.

The silence purifies me,
Washing me clean
Like the ocean over the mammoth rocks

In the emptiness of my mind,
My Spirit soars…
Setting me free.

Divine Mother,

Help me feel the nurturing Spirit

Within all things,

So the fear shadows

That stand like sentinels

Over my soul

Will fly away.

O Blessed Father Sprit,

Fan the flame of my soul

Until I am consumed by the Love-Light

That I am in You.

Divine Mother has invited me

To a feast of tulips, nectar and sunshine.

The tulips are Her gift of beauty,

The nectar Her Divine Love.

And Her Sun is forever shining

On the feast of our union as *ONE*.

FROM THE MOTHER

O my daughter,
Let me carry you on My wings,
For in your walking, you stumble.
In your clinging to the Earth, you fall.

Have no fear, my Beloved
And do not be weary.
Remember, it was I who birthed you.
Trust me now also to carry you.

Walk not on the dry ground,
Seek not the barren tree.
Let us go to the fertile fields,
Child of my longing.

Let us discover together
What Love can create.

THE MUSIC

The music plays, and I begin to know
The place of my innocence.
I feel the stream of love
Coursing through my body,
Awakening my cells to joy and truth.

The peace takes me to another place
Where time fades away
And all familiar scenes are gone.

I am washed in glorious light,
Dancing, always dancing
In my forever soul
Through endless passages
Of unlimited life...

In the journey
Where the music takes me.

29

STILL TIME TO DREAM

Piercing through the silence

Of a thousand dreams,

The Master comes,

Blessing all who reach for "Heaven's gate"…

Giving love and knowledge

That it is not too late.

"There is still time to dream

And feast upon that joy,

Fulfilled in ways that are unknown

Until they are full-birthed,

And dancing at your feet."

SPIRIT'S SONG TO YOU

I can give you sunshine on a rainy day...

I can give you LOVE when you think it's gone away.

I can bring you laughter when my JOY seems not in sight.

I can give you comfort in your darkest night.

And if you feel you cannot move, I'll give you wings to fly.

For I AM the SPIRIT deep within you...

Always with you,

For I AM you,

And I can never die.

THE BLESSING SEED

When I awake each morning,
I bless the birds that call…
I bless the love and light I feel
To be felt by all.

I bless the Earth in living,
With thanks for all the giving.
From the Lord God of my Being,
I God-Bless every one.

I bless this holy instant
Of life pulsing through my soul.
I bless each cell within my body
To be well and whole.

I bless the sweetness of the flowers
To be all they can be.
I bless all the creatures,
And know that they bless me.

I see all curses that once fell
From the lips of a raging soul,
Dissolved into the love and truth
That all is well and whole.

May all who walk Earth's pathways
Find a blessing here indeed;
And find their souls awakening
Within the blessing seed.

MY PRAYER IS

To leave all illusions behind me,

To laugh in the face of the storm,

To know trouble cannot find me

Or anything do me harm.

To dance my full jubilation,

To rest in the peace of the ONE,

To let understanding flow through me,

So that all judgment is gone.

THE KEEPER OF JOY

O my Beloved God,
Let me be the keeper of Your JOY.
Let it overflow in my soul
So that all be lifted where I go.

Let me keep it in my cells
So that they be happy and immortal
In their growth and eternal youthfulness.

Let me keep it in my brain
To keep my body and my life moving
Ever onward into the great expanding joy
Of forever.

O my Beloved God,
Let me be the keeper of Your *JOY*!

PRAYER FOR THE JOURNEY

My Beloved Almighty Holy Spirit,
The mighty wings of Your Love
Are caressing my soul.
In that Love is the remembrance
Of who I am in You
In me.

My Beloved Holy, Holy, Spirit,
Who runs to embrace yourself in me,
My arms are always open…
My soul quivering in your Love,
Shared in the fullness of freedom
Of dreams waking.

We are dancing in the light
Of new creation
At the dawning of this, our journey
Into the unknown joy
Of all that we are together in the dancing
Into the golden laughter of the *ONE*.

When we are *OPEN* and thirsty,
The water of life bubbles up
From the well of joy inside us,
And the blessings of God surround us.

❀ ❀ ❀

HAPPINESS
Is the natural state
Of the human being.

❀ ❀ ❀

God is the chessman
Who plays the *GAME OF LIFE*,
But it is up to us
To say to the God within,
"It's your move."

❀ ❀ ❀

MISPERCEPTION is the great deceiver…
It can create the illusion that
The Earth is a painful place to walk,
When the truth is
There are thorns in the bottom
Of our own shoes.

LIFE can only be in the present.
The past is but a memory,
Masquerading as the truth.

❀ ❀ ❀

It does not matter where your body is.
It only matters where your *MIND* is.

❀ ❀ ❀

We will know we have manifested *ONENESS*
When we are both hungry,
But I give my food to you…
And as you eat,
I am filled.

❀ ❀ ❀

Miracles push their way up
Through our *WILLINGNESS*.

❀ ❀ ❀

WORK is worship
When we remember the sacredness
Of all things and people.

❀ ❀ ❀

The carpenter works with *JOY*,
Remembering
He is not just pounding a nail.
He is building a house.

This *DREAM* we created
Is like a maze of mirrors
Reflecting back to us
That which we think we are.

❀ ❀ ❀

To complete our earthly journey
Without repetition,
We need only change our *ATTITUDES*.

❀ ❀ ❀

The path of surrender
Includes the release
Of all *JUDGMENTS*.

❀ ❀ ❀

It takes only one *MOVEMENT*
To help everything else move.
It does not matter what or how.
One pebble dropped into the ocean
Changes it forever.

❀ ❀ ❀

True *WISDOM* comes
When we surrender our opinions
And everything we think we know
At the feet of the Divine Master within.

❀ ❀ ❀

Clear *VISION* belongs to the one
Who sees no duality.

DESIRE AND EMOTION
Bring conception and manifestation.

❀   ❀   ❀

WISDOM AND UNDERSTANDING
Come after emotions are fully felt.

❀   ❀   ❀

True *WISDOM* questions everything
That does not feel loving.

❀   ❀   ❀

A *JUDGMENT* is any thought
That separates us from each other.

❀   ❀   ❀

THIS JOURNEY is not forever,
For one day all will remember
What we chose to forget.

❀   ❀   ❀

The ocean is laughing…
The sky is happy.
The earth beneath our feet is dancing!
Why do you weep?

❀   ❀   ❀

In the all that there is to know and be,
I AM.

THE JOURNEY AND THE PROMISE

We have dipped our feet
In the fountain of dreams
To swim in the river of life.
We have played victim and tyrant,
The child, the husband, the wife.

We have clothed ourselves
With the shades of red,
Of black, of yellow and white.
We have shed the cloak of evenness
For a garment of wrong and right.

But the wise ones say
That the journey through time
Will end and a new Kingdom come,
As our souls awaken from the dream
To return to the *PEACE* of the *ONE*.

This poem is included in the "Longest Poem for Peace" that was presented by the International Society of Poets to the United Nations in a ceremony during the 1993 winter holidays. Iris Arla Moore was inducted into this organization that same year. It is the desire of all of us that you join us in choosing PEACE inside yourself; that it bless and hasten PEACE in the entire World.

JUDGMENT

Finally,

Judgment that had eaten away at my soul

Like a cancer,

Rose like the phoenix;

Transmuted into wisdom,

With a new vision

Of the ongoing beginnings

And the ongoing endings

Of life in love with itself.

LIFE IS A JOURNEY

Life is a journey to find all the pieces;
To learn, and to listen to the feelings that call.
Life is a turning from one place to another,
As we trust and we follow the tide in us all.

Sometimes we walk in the shadows of knowing
That while on the journey, we're already there…
And while we are watching the things all around us,
We feel we are part of all that we share.

Life is a resting in the grace and the loving
That carries us into who we are and can be.
Life is embracing all that comes to us;
To feel in each moment that we are free.

THE DANCE OF PERSPECTIVE

ONE MAN'S SUNSET
IS ANOTHER'S SUNRISE,
AS WE DANCE THROUGH THE CHANGES
THAT MOVE THROUGH OUR LIVES.

IT'S THE DANCE OF PERSPECTIVE,
THE DESIRE TO SEE
WHO BE YOU AND WHO BE ME.

IT'S LETTING GO OF ILLUSIONS,
AND SEEING WHAT'S TRUE:
THE SPIRIT IN ME AND THE SPIRIT IN YOU...

TO FINALLY REALIZE ALL IS ONE:
THE OBSERVER, THE OCEAN, THE SAND AND THE SUN.

CHANGE

It is only a breath away...
This gigantic miracle of change
To freedom, peace and love
Pervading all.

In only a moment,
It will seem that the treacherous past
Never existed,
As only love remains
After we walked through centuries
And dung heaps of illusions,
Believing them to be real.

Om Shanti, Om Shanti...
Peace at last has caught up with me,
Since I have stopped the running
From fear
That had turned love upside down.

Now I see clearly
Through eyes of understanding and hope,
Finally remembering
All there ever was
Is *LOVE* making known the unknown

THE   BRIDGE

The pale moon waits

Over the bridge to tomorrow,

Knowing it soon will reflect

The full glory of the sun.

My heart is racing to meet you there

By the water's edge

When the new dawn comes

To lead us all into the splendor

That we are

In the Love remembered.

ABOUT THE AUTHOR

Iris Arla Moore has written poetry since age twelve. It was then that the sudden, unexpected death of her mother caused a severe emotional shock to her brain. After this, she had a spiritual awakening, felt her connection to the spirit, and began writing poetry that flowed through her like a river running.

Her spiritual journey includes many spiritual healing therapies and trainings. First was Self-Realization Fellowship, which led to amazing experiences with the immortal master, Haidakhandi Babaji, in India. A Course In Miracles was next. The last several years, she has been a student at a modern school of ancient wisdom: Ramtha's School of Enlightenment .

This author has received local and International honors for her poetry. She has also written and published a beautiful and delightful children's picture book (for all ages)—a true story about a pet bantam hen in an auto shop. Henrietta the Guard Chicken has the magic to bond the soul to unconditional love.

BENEDICTION

Gentle be your journey...
Light for the way,
Happiness always
And peace that will stay.
Om...